Contents

2ND EDITION

Achieving Success in GOLF

Success in hitting a good golf shot is often inversely proportional to the number of thoughts in your head during the swing

STRAW DOG

PREFACE

Here are some pages on golf, an amazing sport. The main purpose of these pages is to have you be kind to yourself, even be a friend to yourself.

Secondarily, the following sentences and sketches are designed to help you understand the game, and from that foundation, conquer a challenging sport.

There are zillions of fine publications and books on golf. If this collection of thoughts on paper gets thick enough to be called a book, then I have failed. It is gonna be just a booklet. As you are reading the sentences of the booklet and seeing the sketches, I hope that you have a "duh" or "really?" moment as you instantly understand the building-block concepts that you can quickly turn into beneficial tools in your quest to gain mastery of this sport.

THE GAME

Tennis is a fabulous sport, but if 2 people have different abilities, then they may have some challenges in playing each other. If you have 4 people of different abilities in golf, different backgrounds, even of different parts of the world-maybe even speak different languages- then you have a foursome. Golf can help you meet lots of fine people, visit beautiful places, and get some exercise. Even a person with poor success in all other sports can play golf well (equipment is fabulous). (Even just going to a driving range and whacking a golf ball can be cathartic and fun).

The CHALLENGE

Golf is typically not an easy game to learn. A great article was published in the January 29, 2014 Wall Street Journal: "Whoever Said Golf Was Supposed to Be Fun?"

> *Is learning the violin fun? Is becoming a competitive chess player fun? Minigolf, with its colored balls and Ferris wheels, is fun. But the satisfaction derived from real golf is much more profound than the word "fun" would suggest... Golf is beyond fun: It is the ultimate sporting test of physical coordination, mental focus, strategy and nerves... "It takes a special kind of person to play golf" ... Face it, the sport is cruel.*

> -Christian Chensvold

For men, golf seems so tied to ego. Typically, the game is done in public and wow, it can be punishing/ humiliating. (Women have the ability to more readily laugh at the game). So, lots of people will not voluntarily go through the usually necessary, brutal, early learning curves.

One important purpose of this booklet is to replace GIP (Golf Induced Pain) with GAPE (Golf Associated Pleasure and Enjoyment).

THINKING

This booklet does not say thinking is bad-quite the opposite. Golf invites and challenges you to learn and think about so many facets regarding a wonderful endeavor. Read books and magazines. Take lessons from a pro. Nevertheless, when you are hitting a shot, then I contend that the more thoughts in your head, the harder it is to hit the ball well. YES, there is definitely the importance of understanding and doing the (non-thinking) setup.

- The Grip

- The Equipment

- The Mechanics

- The Stance

However, during your actual swing, I want you to actively think of only about 2 things (these to be covered later, after discussion of components of the SETUP).

SETUP

The Grip

Most books out there have excellent diagrams about the grip. I think that in a simple statement-have the "V"s (V formed by the thumb and index finger) go toward the right shoulder.

Chick Evans Golf Book (Copyright Expired)

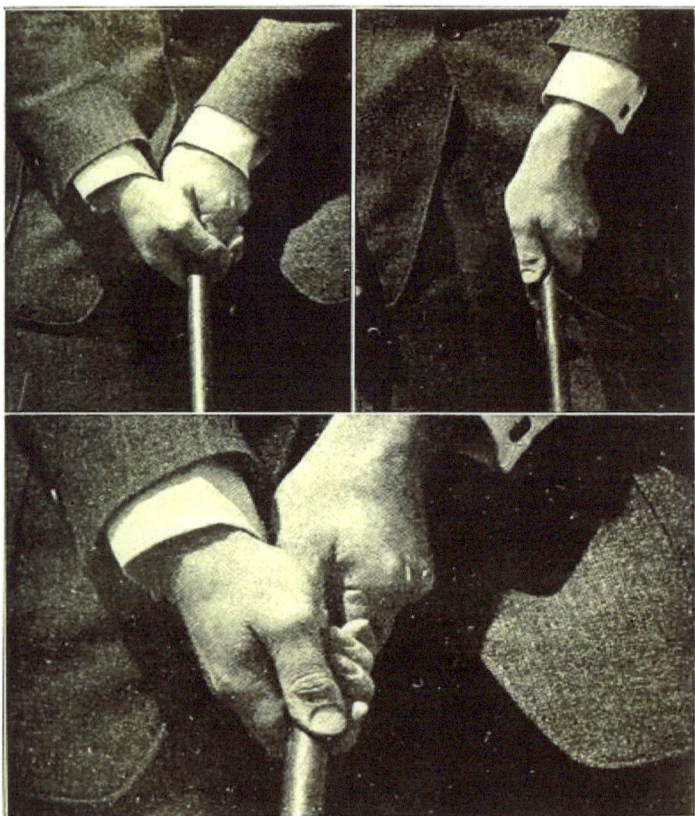

The Equipment

Equipment these days is fabulous. When I started playing half a century ago, it was not nearly as good. Some years back when my kids started playing the game, I bought a new set of clubs for them: 4 woods and 9 irons, all with graphite shafts, for about $200- and I tried them out and found them to be basically the same wonderful technology as my name brand, more expensive set. Yes, ideally, go to a pro and have a fitting to help you with proper flex and shaft length- but hey, take any available set- from a relative, garage sale, you name it, and go to a driving range. (One of the biggest problems to watch out for is *slick* grips. Slick grips will wreck your experience and are a common problem. It is very affordable to have new grips put on).

The Mechanics

Here are some basic ideas. (No, I'm not gonna call it physics, because I refuse to make it sound formidable).

Spin

Your golf shot is determined in a fraction of a second- when the ball hits the clubface (moment of destiny/ truth). OK, so if it spins to the right, then it will fly to the right. If it spins left, then it will fly to the left. If it has topspin (also called overspin), it will tend to dive downward, and reverse spin (backspin), will tend to make it go up. This may be a simplified way to picture it, but these principles will let you master the fundamentals of the game.

Club Face

One of the differences between clubs is the design of the clubface, which correlates with the point in the swing where the clubface should impact the ball. Loftier clubs (shorter irons, higher numbers) require you to hit down on the ball, hitting the ball before the lowest part of the swing. The impact imparts backspin and that, with the loft of the face, tends to make the ball go up. As the clubs get shorter (the clubface loftier), the more you hit down on the ball. Even a 3 wood and the long irons should strike the ball before the bottom of the swing. A driver has a nearly vertical face, and it is probably the only club with which you hit the ball on the upswing (hence use of a tee). It creates some overspin, and potentially sidespin. Dimples create the aerodynamic benefits of having the ball fly in a straight trajectory rather than all over the place (a ball without dimples would probably be fun to hit on a range).

Desired Impact Zones

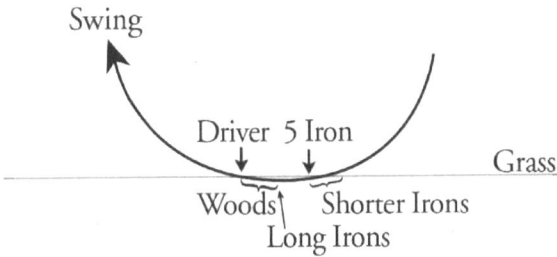

Spin Applications

If you get "ahead of the ball" with your hands (body usually too far forward), then the club face opens, and the ball is cut across, imparting right spin, so the ball goes to the right (fades and slices, proportionate to the "infraction"). Another, though mechanically different, cause of right spin is an outside – in club swing path (and you can envision how that makes the clubface cut across the ball). A third cause of right spin is to have a "weak right hand" (think of the right hand moving in position to be more under the club grip, where the "V" points to the right of the right shoulder). Reverse any of these processes and a left spin results with the ball flying to the left.

Equipment Note:

If your club face has poor alignment-either pointing

in (closed) or out (open), then that will cause undesired spin, and that can be easily fixed.

Stance

Let's face it- you now already know a lot, and many fundamentals are now your friends, not strangers in a dark alley. Feet position-

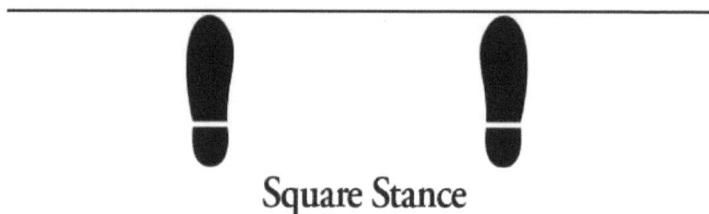

Square Stance

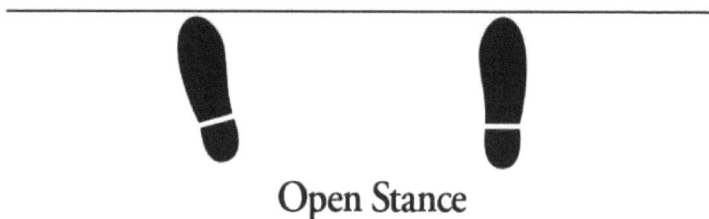

Open Stance

An open stance, I think, makes swing delivery smoother and easier, particularly for shorter irons (not as important, for instance, for woods).

Ball Position

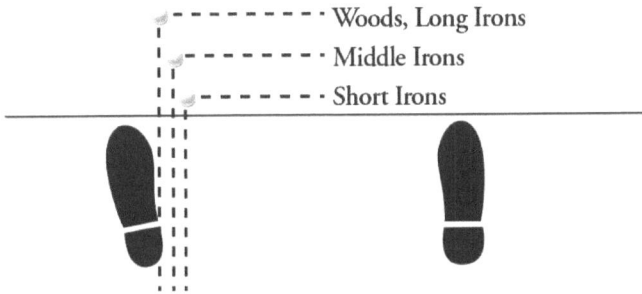

Woods, Long Irons
Middle Irons
Short Irons

Decades ago, there was the thought of gradually playing clubs back toward the middle of the stance, as the clubs got shorter. Instead, I think a better approach is playing all clubs more toward the inner part of the left foot. Honestly, mechanically, I do think this permits easier delivery of energy/weight behind the ball.

Alignment

As you are addressing the ball, consider laying one or two clubs down parallel to your proposed line of flight. Often, you may be surprised. This is an easy and very helpful tool.

Rotation

Turn like you are in a barrel. Do not laterally sway.

Knee Position

I never think about it.

Feet Motion

I never think about it, but it seems that at the top of my swing, my left heel comes off the ground some, and during follow-through, my right heel comes up some.

Head Position

Your head should be a pretty fixed point and looking at the ball- probably not at planes or birds overhead.

Now, we come to the actual (second) purpose of this book. (Remember, the first purpose of the book is to be nice to yourself- patient/kind for example, as you are learning-not calling yourself names or giving a **** what other people think).

At this point, you have the SETUP thought out and completed, and now I stress that I don't want much (thinking) "noise" in your head during your entire swing. We will focus on only (2) crucial thinking points (this creates smoothness and clarity).

FIRST THINKING POINT: TEMPO

Take the club back with deliberate SLOWNESS (should feel odd) only to a STRAIGHT LEFT ARM (although can bend the wrists some at the top). I have found that the exact degree to which I bend my left arm is proportional to the degree I get ahead of the ball and thereby make the club face open (so, I then lose power, accuracy and right spin makes the ball go to the right). (One book has a 5th and final point saying, "start your downswing with your hips." To me that pretty much guarantees that my body will be ahead of the ball at impact; instead, I think the hands should begin the downswing).

SECOND THINKING POINT: IMPACT PLANE

So now, let's get on to the Second Thinking Point: imagine a pane of glass that you are hitting squarely against. It goes vertically from the inner left foot to the inner left knee and up about your left armpit and left ear.

At impact, you want most of your body weight behind the pane of glass, or plane, and your hands square to it- for if you are in front of it, then your hands will be in front of it, and you will lose power and have all the problems associated with an open club face.

So, the two points to think about: take the club back as slowly as you can stand (backswing: slowly count – one and two…. Then three for the downswing (some people find it helpful to actually pause momentarily at the top))- up to the straight left arm, and then deliver the club face squarely into the impact zone while keeping the majority of the body weight strategically behind the IMPACT PLANE.

Chipping Around the Green

A chipping iron can really offer finesse. It is essentially a putter with a club face with a small amount of loft. To me, it offers a great deal of feel, much like a putter and can be used with a shortened stroke, as opposed to a bladed club.

Putting

Obviously, a great student of putting, a person named Pelz wrote a big book on the subject. Two key ideas stuck with me:

1. "The difference between a good putter and a great putter is about a million practice strokes."
2. He also spoke of the advantages of a long putter.

A couple of years ago, I went to a golf shop and saw a 40-inch belly putter (Power Bilt EX200 MA330). The first round was not good, but since then, it has really transformed my putting in a good way. I see 3 advantages:

1. I can stand up much better and actually visualize the hole when I'm putting. This is a huge benefit rather than putting blindly in the usual bent over posture (even hurts my back).
2. For some reason seems to impart a topspin roll, and I think a topspin roll rolls truer. (Anyone ever study a topspin roll)?
3. It takes my wrists out of the stroke.

I want to briefly mention what I will call the "punishment angle." It is the triangle at the club face where the putter face does not exactly follow the exact line to the hole. This angle ain't my friend. The bigger the angle the more likely I will miss the putt. And Likely Miss (LM) is the distance that increases the longer the putt, making it more likely to miss the putt. By using a belly putter, I get more of a pendulum stroke and take my wrists out of the equation. (I do not anchor the putter on my belly. Also for me, the longer "broomstick" putters do not work). Making putts has increased my enjoyment of the game.

BLUE ICE PEARL #1

(Keep Your Eyes on the Prize)

I have always been, at best, an average putter. I'm 70 years old and yes, my golf library is about 6 feet wide. I have read and studied ALL aspects of the game and since putting accounts for a disproportionate part of the final score, I have practiced putting extensively for over half a century. Still at best, I am an average putter. (As mentioned earlier in the text, a belly putter has really helped me). To me, there is nothing more unnerving than a missing a short putt (no wait a minute, there are lots of unnerving things about golf).

BUT RECENTLY, I have made a breakthrough!

I have had the same insurance agent, Kim, for about a dozen years. He is retirement age, but when I ask a rare question, he is often in his office – impressive dedication, staff always too - he comes up with answers quickly. It is a friendship. So naturally, some years ago when I was visiting his office, we started talking about golf. He told me that when he putts, he only looks at the hole.

I immediately dismissed it: "Absurd, Preposterous-Pure Nuttiness," I thought. His idea goes against all the putting techniques/tenets I have utilized for decades!

But a few weeks ago, I thought I would try it! If I do not look at the ball and have the face of the putter centered at impact, isn't that a recipe for ugliness? And the level of the club- won't I top it and sometimes scuff it?

So, I had a "Leap of Faith" (I always liked the imagery of Indiana Jones stepping into thin air over the fiery lava, and the bridge appeared under his feet).

I do not look at the ball or putter AT ALL when I putt! I oddly do not mishit it. I have a panoramic, 3-D view of the line. Wonderful! I judge distances far better and see the break(s) better. For shorter putts, I have the ball die at the hole, so I can use the entire cup.

Another key thing: I more automatically stroke through the ball along the intended line of roll. (One of my previous big flaws was to quit on the putting stroke shortly after the impact.)

Like all my pursuits of all aspects of golf, I'm still studying it.

This technique, to me, works best of putts under 5 feet – also, very beneficial of putts of up to 10-15 feet; however, I'm not so sure for putts over 20-25 feet – maybe then, because good impact with the middle of the putter face is so crucial, more conventional putting techniques should be employed.

Blue Ice Pearl #2:

The snow is going to start flying soon, so my wife and I went out last night to play one of our last rounds of the year.

I thank my dad for helping me learn the great game of golf. I had some of his important words come back to me last night (when he wasn't telling me to get a haircut and get a job), "keep your right elbow in at the top of the swing." I added it to the 2 Thinking Points discussed previously. It does seem to make the swing more compact and reproducible. To me, tucking the right elbow in comfortably at the top of the swing mechanically contributes to power and accuracy.

So, 2 different definitions of "blue ice" in stark contrast:

1). Emphasizing the beautiful blue color that comes form the purest ice on the entire planet.

VS.

2). The color of the blue dye colored ice stuck on the outside of a jet airplane on the drain valve that serves the lavatory. I hope you will try this **BOLD** putting technique – it may be **BEAUTIFUL** – or maybe something else...

SUMMARY

Think of a graceful, even spiritual swing. Golf loves to have its parables/paradoxes-the faster and harder I swing, the less power I will have and less accuracy. Think too of smoothness and tempo.

Be able to laugh at the game (even a little in a healthy fashion at yourself- but probably ought to not laugh at other people). Always think of having Alfred E. Neuman in your group.

Be kind and patient with yourself. Often, we would never allow a stranger to treat us like we treat ourselves. From being nice to yourself, you then find it easier to be nicer to those around you.

Learn about the game. Read books, magazines, and whatever about it that gives you enjoyment. Take lessons. Enjoy nature and the people you encounter along the way.

Beware that golf can be selfish- don't let it steal you away from more valuable stuff (like family, health, etc... but properly conducted, it can enhance family, health, etc...).

Hopefully this booklet can help you rapidly gain initial proficiency in golf and quickly and dramatically replace GIP with GAPE.

My only goal all along is for you to "Enjoy the Game of Golf", (see also: "Yippee ki-Yay").

Sincerely,
Straw Dog

BOOK CITATIONS

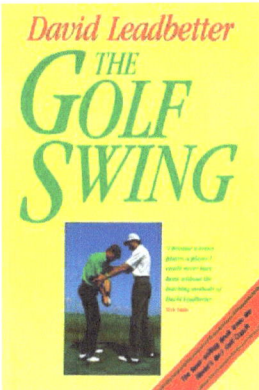

Leadbetter, David. The Golf Swing. United States: The Stephen Greene Press, 1990. Print.

Fabulous book, great diagrams wonderful 5-page summary. Still, I think the bulk of the book is best suited for the advanced beginner and beyond.

Cochran, Alastair, and John Stobbs. Search for the Perfect Swing: The Proven Scientific Approach to Fundamentally Improving Your Game. The Golf Society of Great Britain, 1968. Print.

Wonderful-particularly for the scientific geeks who like science/physics. If I could copy pages for the booklet, it would be the photo sequences of two golfers who only had a left arm. Perfect fundamentals. Permission to copy book cover requested and pending.

Obetz, Christopher, and Anthony Ravielli. 100 Classic Golf Tips from Leading Ladies' Teaching and Touring Pros. Universe Publishing, 2008.

Wonderful. Women often display graceful finesse in the game (Often more exemplary behavior). She represents a perfect illustration of the top of the swing – the left arm straight! Permission to copy book cover requested and pending.

Morelli, Jay. 365 Golf Tips & Tricks From the Pros. New York: Sterling Publishing, 2013.

Was it Rachmaninoff who said something like, "The horizons in music keep settling in the distance"? Golf is whatever you want it to be in the terms of understanding/challenges. Permission to copy book cover requested and pending.

TERMS:

Alfred E. Neuman is the fictitious mascot of the American humor magazine *Mad*.

Yippee ki-yay

According to Wikipedia, the exclamation "yippee ki yay" is a cowboy term that originated in the 19th century. The earliest known record of the phrase is from Sinclair Lewis's 1920 novel Main Street. The phrase was reimagined for the 1988 movie starring Bruce Willis.

The word "yippee" is used to express excitement, happiness, or great satisfaction. The earliest known use of the word "yippee" is in the 1920's, but its origin is uncertain.

"Yippee." *Merriam-Webster.com Dictionary*, **Merriam-Webster, https://www.merriam-webster.com/dictionary/yippee. Accessed 28 Sep. 2024**. (The phrase "Yippie ki-Yay" it seemingly derives from "yippie yi yo kayah," a refrain from a 1930s Bing Crosby song, "I'm An Old Cowhand." (Also, it was popularized by cowboy actor Roy Rogers's own "Yippee-ki-yah, kids" on The Roy Rogers Show of the 1950s; also reference the Die Hard movie franchise, in which actor Bruce Willis popularized the statement "Yippie Ki Yay, ***********) into a catchphrase.))

Blue ice (glacial)

Blue ice occurs when snow falls on a glacier, is compressed, and becomes part of the glacier. During compression, air bubbles are squeezed out, so ice crystals enlarge. This enlargement is responsible for the ice's blue colour.

Small amounts of regular ice appear to be white because of air bubbles inside and also because small quantities of water appear to be colourless. In glaciers, the pressure causes the air bubbles to be squeezed out, increasing the density of the created ice. Water is blue in large quantities, as it absorbs other colours more efficiently than blue. A large piece of compressed ice, or a glacier, similarly appears blue.

The blue color is sometimes wrongly attributed to Rayleigh scattering, which is responsible for the color of the sky. Rather, water ice is blue for the same reason that large quantities of liquid water are blue: it is a result of an overtone of an oxygen–hydrogen (O–H) bond stretch in water, which absorbs light at the red end of the visible spectrum.[1] So, water owes its intrinsic blueness (as seen after > 3 meters of penetration) to selective absorption in the red part of its visible spectrum. The absorbed photons drive vibrational (normally infrared) transitions.

Once blue ice is exposed to warmer air, cracks and fissures appear in surface layers, and break up the large blue crystals of dense, pure ice. Within hours these air filled fissures cloud the surface making the ice appear white. The blue colour will not be seen again until the ice breaks or turns over to expose ice which air could not reach. For example, lucky tourists at <u>Tasman Glacier</u>, <u>New Zealand</u> in January 2011 saw an iceberg roll over to reveal startling blue ice, kept from air by staying underwater for months since the iceberg calved.[2]

Antarctic runways

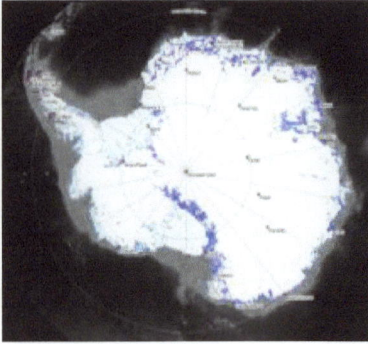

Blue ice fields in Antarctica

Blue ice is exposed in areas of the Antarctic where there is no net addition or subtraction of snow. That is, any snow that falls in that area is counteracted by sublimation or other losses. Such areas are known as blue-ice areas.[3] These areas have been used as runways (e.g. Wilkins Runway,

Novolazarevskaya, Patriot Hills Base Camp) due to their hard surface, which is suitable for aircraft fitted with wheels rather than skis.

References

1. ^ Braun, Charles L.; Smirnov, Sergei N. (August 1993). _"Why Is Water Blue?"_. _J. Chem. Edu._, 1993, 70(8), 612. _Dartmouth College_. Archived from _the original_ on 2012-03-20. Retrieved 2013-12-22.

2. ^ Harvey, Eveline (14 January 2011). _"NZ blue ice sighting an unexpected treat for tourists"_. _The New Zealand Herald_. Retrieved 21 September 2011.

3. ^ Laybourn-Parry, Johanna; Wadham, Jemma (2014-08-14). _Antarctic Lakes_. OUP Oxford. _ISBN_ _9780191649325_.

Blue ice (aviation)

From Wikipedia, the free encyclopedia

In aviation, blue ice is frozen sewage material that has leaked mid-flight from commercial aircraft lavatory waste systems. It is a mixture of human biowaste and liquid disinfectant that freezes at high altitude. The name comes from the blue color of the disinfectant. Airlines are not allowed to dump their waste tanks mid-flight, and pilots have no mechanism by which to do so;[1] however, leaks sometimes do occur from a plane's septic tank.

Danger of ground impact

There were at least 27 documented incidents of blue ice impacts in the United States between 1979 and 2003.[2] These incidents typically happen under airport landing paths as the mass warms sufficiently to detach from the plane during its descent. A rare incident of falling blue ice causing damage to the roof of a home was reported on October 20, 2006 in Chino, California.[3] A similar incident was reported in Leicester, UK, in 2007.[4]

References

1. ^ Chandra, Neha (18 September 2018). *"Fact File: Do aircraft really drop poop from sky?"*. *India Today*. Retrieved 2023-02-26.
2. ^ Gumz, Jondi (February 12, 2003). *"Another mysterious chunk of blue ice hits"*. *Santa Cruz Sentinel*.
6. ^ *"'Football-sized' ice smashes home"*. *BBC News*. February 11, 2013. Retrieved 2017-07-26.

7. **^** *Naveen, P. "Pnaen dropping 'blue ice' can be indentified from radar images".* Times of India. Retrieved 30 September 2024.

8. **^** *"Meteoriet blijkt drol uit vliegtuig".* Retrieved 2016-10-31.

14. ^ Jump up to:*[a] [b] [c] "January 04, 1990 Incident".* NTSB. Retrieved 2011-04-16.

15.**^** *Derek Elley (October 14, 1992). "Blue Ice Review". Variety. Retrieved 2009-03-26.*

CREDITS

The author, Straw Dog (Hoosier-Hawaiian name), has really no golf credentials but has a background of lots of formal book learning and having read lots of information on golf. The game has taken me to many beautiful places and has allowed me to meet countless fine people and have a lot of enjoyment.

Thanks go to Don. He started playing about 6 years ago and initially, I thought no one was safe around him for 360 degrees. He would miss a shot and instead of getting mad, he would laugh and put down another ball. We would play in off times so we could look for golf balls ("operation reload"). One time he went in a woods and disappeared. I was wondering if I needed to put his picture on a milk carton or if he joined the camera crew of National Geographic looking for a stone age tribe. Then, he came out of a clearing, his white pants covered in mud and with so many golf balls in his pockets that he looked like a mutant. Now, he plays great (problem is now he hits a shot and just freezes, admiring it, and I have to tell him we need to move on). Thanks Don for showing me that humor really must be a healthy part of the game.

And then there is Charlie, my bro-in-law. When we played 35 years ago, I was in the part of my life where I played a lot. He did not play that well.

Beam forward a bunch of years: I gave away about 30 copies of Leadbetter's book. He may have been the only one to really read it, and it was his springboard. Now, he has a golf swing that could be a teaching video. I kept thinking- why do I like his swing so much? The tempo (so important) was so smooth, and there seemed to be so few moving parts. He really helped me clearly see a beautiful display of the fundamentals. Thanks Charlie.

And my Hawaiian Ohana: Del, Ellie, Dave, and Terri. Del gave me my Hawaiian name. Thirty-five years ago, I played a lot of golf with Del. I'd hit a drive, and then he would hit. "Givem". He would almost always outdrive me. Pure Aloha.

Heaven gave me my wife, Barbara, and Russell, Whitney, Gracie, and Emerson. Extra thanks go to Barbara, Whitney, and Russell for help with edits.

Pure shouts of Thanks to God, my Pal. He manages to help keep me in the fairway of life, and I'm always on the watch for His beauty.

Oh, I have mentioned some books and a club above. No, I have not received any endorsement money. Later though, if you see me covered with stickers and

30 pounds of decals on my hat, you can ask if anything has changed.